THE MAGIC OF SOUND

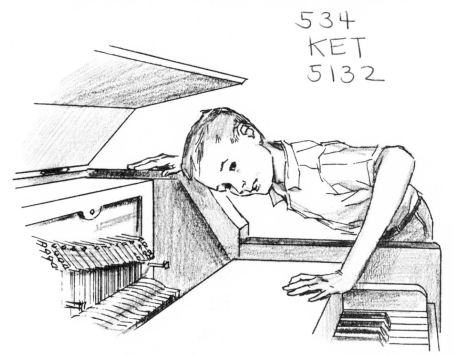

written and illustrated by
LARRY KETTELKAMP

WILLIAM MORROW and COMPANY · New York · 1956

Grateful recognition is given to J. T. Tykociner, Research Professor Emeritus of Electrical Engineering, University of Illinois, Urbana, Illinois, for his helpful suggestions.

· · · · · · · · ·

CONTENTS

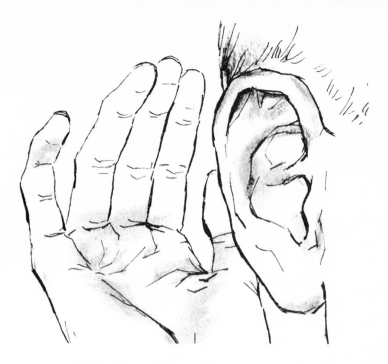

Producing Sounds

Sounds are very curious. You cannot touch them and you cannot see them. But it is impossible to imagine what our lives would be like without the use of speech, the joy of laughter, or the beauty of music. Because sound is so important to us, it will be interesting to try some experiments that can help us understand what sounds are and how they work.

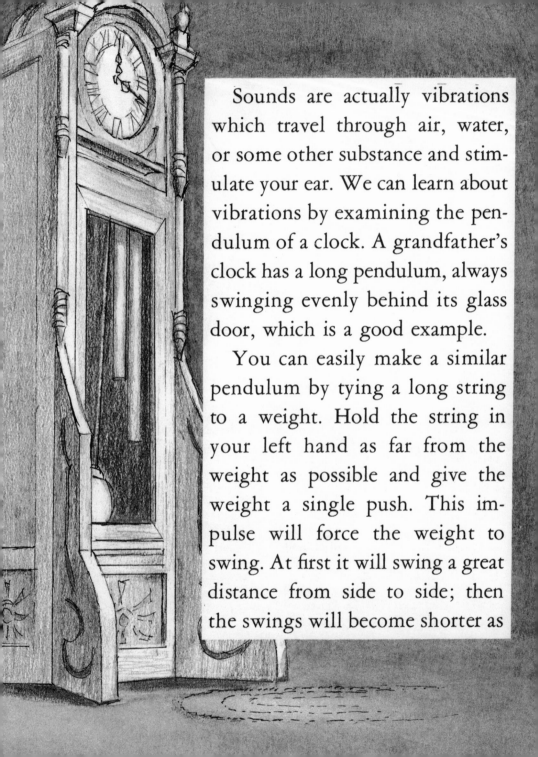

Sounds are actually vibrations which travel through air, water, or some other substance and stimulate your ear. We can learn about vibrations by examining the pendulum of a clock. A grandfather's clock has a long pendulum, always swinging evenly behind its glass door, which is a good example.

You can easily make a similar pendulum by tying a long string to a weight. Hold the string in your left hand as far from the weight as possible and give the weight a single push. This impulse will force the weight to swing. At first it will swing a great distance from side to side; then the swings will become shorter as

the weight's momentum decreases. Each time
it passes in front of you, count its swing. All
counts will be in the same slow, even time,
whether the weight is swinging in a wide arc or
in a short one. Now hold the string closer to
the weight. Your counting will be faster but
still in even time. The shorter the string, the
faster the pendulum will swing.

It is just such a back-and-forth movement, often invisible, that produces the sounds we hear. But the pendulum would have to move back and forth about twenty times per second in air to produce an audible tone. We do not hear a continuous tone if the movements are less frequent than this. These back-and-forth

IF THE PENDULUM COULD MOVE BACK AND FORTH ABOUT 41 TIMES PER SECOND, IT MIGHT SOUND LIKE THE LOWEST NOTE OF THE STRING BASS

movements are called vibrations. Our ears can hear a tone caused by as many as 15,000 vibrations in one second.

To understand how these vibrations affect our ears, try a stunt with a deck of cards. Arrange the cards so that they overlap in a row, and give the bottom card a flip. A wavelike

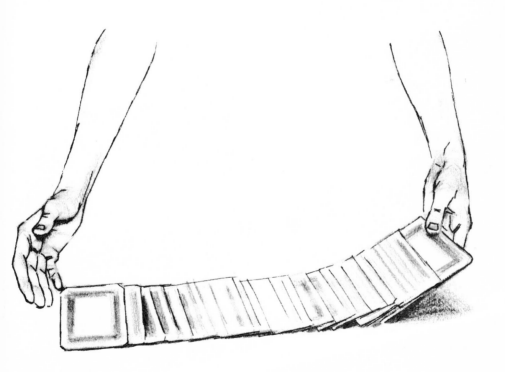

disturbance will travel from card to card down the row. If this could be repeated back and forth many times, it would give the pack of cards a wave motion. Sound travels through the air in much the same way.

The air is made up of many small particles called molecules. When molecules are set into vibration, they excite each other as the cards did in the experiment. If you imagine that the molecules in the air are, like the cards, affected by a push, or a vibration, you will have a good idea of the way sound travels.

When these vibrations reach our ears, they strike a thin sheet of skin inside each of them called an eardrum. The eardrum is so sensitive that it, too, vibrates at the same frequency as the air which excites it. We say that we hear when the effects of these vibrations are transmitted from the eardrum to the brain.

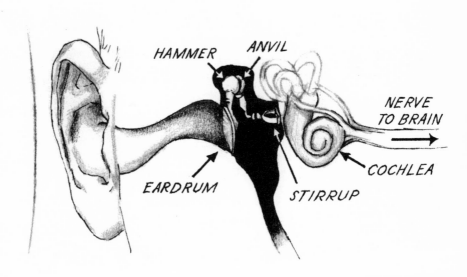

vibrations of the eardrum are transmitted to the brain through the middle ear (the hammer, anvil, and stirrup) and the cochlea

An experiment with a metal cake spatula will teach us more about vibrations. Hold the tip of the spatula blade on the edge of a kitchen table with one hand, and strike its handle with the other. You may hear a low, raspy tone. As you move still more of the blade onto the table, the shorter portion will vibrate faster than the long portion that extended at first. When the vibrations come fast enough to be heard as a single tone, you will find that the pitch of the sound becomes higher as the vibrating part of the spatula grows shorter. The difference between high and low tones is that a high tone is of a greater frequency.

Striking the spatula hard will produce a loud tone while the blade swings in a wide arc. As the arc grows smaller until the blade stops, the volume of the tone also decreases.

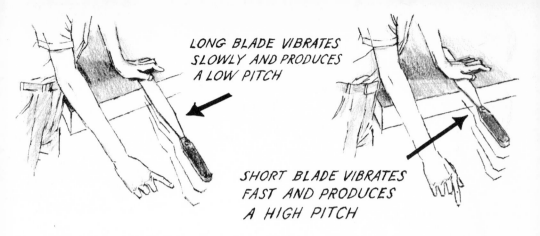

LONG BLADE VIBRATES
SLOWLY AND PRODUCES
A LOW PITCH

SHORT BLADE VIBRATES
FAST AND PRODUCES
A HIGH PITCH

It is possible to draw a picture of a vibration. With your right hand hold a pencil point on a large sheet of paper. Bend your arm at the elbow and swing your hand back and forth, moving the pencil over the paper. Keep the pencil moving evenly as you gradually pull the paper away from you with your left hand. The pencil will trace a wavy line down the page. This is a picture of the vibrations of your arm.

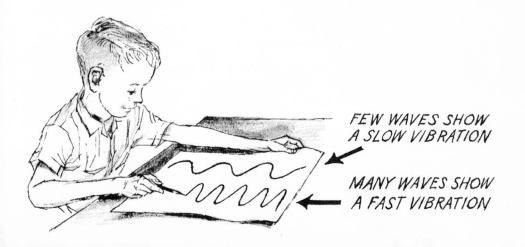

FEW WAVES SHOW
A SLOW VIBRATION

MANY WAVES SHOW
A FAST VIBRATION

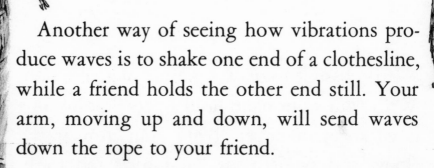

Another way of seeing how vibrations produce waves is to shake one end of a clothesline, while a friend holds the other end still. Your arm, moving up and down, will send waves down the rope to your friend.

Scientists can make any sound wave visible electrically, including those that are too high or too low for our ears to detect, on a machine called an oscilloscope. This machine traces the

OSCILLOSCOPE

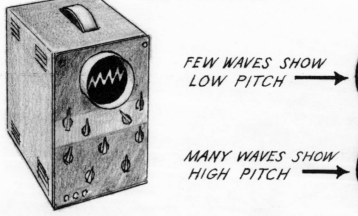

FEW WAVES SHOW
LOW PITCH ➔

MANY WAVES SHOW
HIGH PITCH ➔

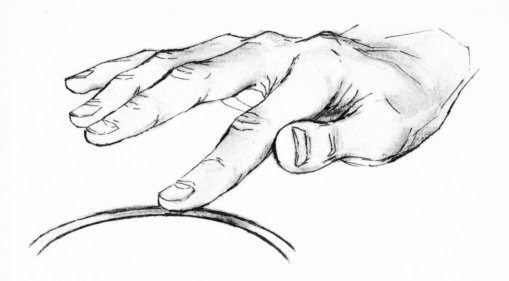

path of sound vibrations by means of an electron beam.

There are many ways to produce musical sounds. Try moistening your finger with a little water and rubbing the rim of a drinking glass slowly and evenly. Soon the tip of your finger will feel tacky and will make small vibrations as it slides around. The glass should sing out with a loud clear note. Your finger makes the glass vibrate just as a violin bow vibrates a string when it moves across it.

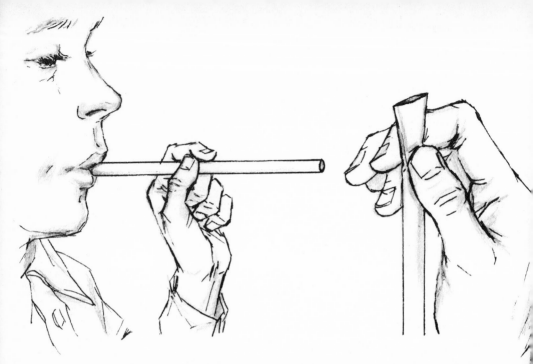

Vibrations can also be made by blowing. Pinch one end of a drinking straw so that it is almost flat. Put the flattened end into your mouth, blow hard, and you will get a good tone. The flattened paper at the end of the straw is vibrated by air pressure from your lungs. Even the air itself can be made to vibrate. When you blow across the top of a pop bottle, the column of air inside the bottle vibrates.

Wonderful musical instruments have been

created by using the same vibrations that have been described. The tones of a flute are produced by blowing across an opening near one end of the tube. The column of air inside the flute vibrates just as the air inside the pop bottle vibrated. Instruments like the clarinet

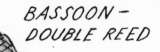

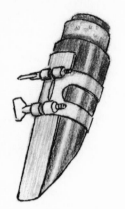

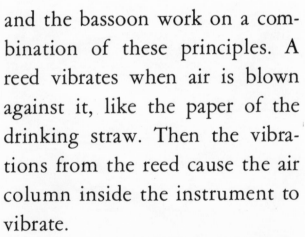

and the bassoon work on a com-
bination of these principles. A
reed vibrates when air is blown
against it, like the paper of the
drinking straw. Then the vibrations from the reed cause the air
column inside the instrument to
vibrate.

Today we hear instruments
with sounds that are made electrically. The tones of an electric

18

organ are produced by making electricity move back and forth at varying speeds, so that it can create a vibration of any pitch. A new electronic instrument called a trautonium is being used with some symphony orchestras. Its tones are new and exciting, because they have never been heard before.

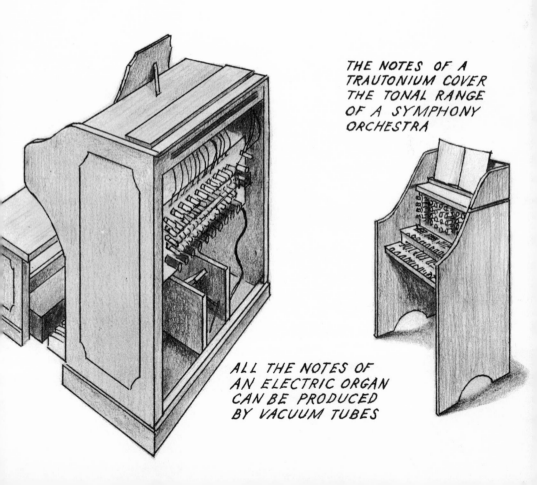

THE NOTES OF A TRAUTONIUM COVER THE TONAL RANGE OF A SYMPHONY ORCHESTRA

ALL THE NOTES OF AN ELECTRIC ORGAN CAN BE PRODUCED BY VACUUM TUBES

Capturing Sounds

Although most of the sounds we hear come to our ears through the air, they do not travel their fastest this way. Sound travels only a little over a thousand feet per second in air.

REFLECTED SUNLIGHT TRAVELS FROM THE MOON TO THE EARTH IN LITTLE MORE THAN A SECOND

LIGHT FROM A FIREWORKS
EXPLOSION REACHES US
ALMOST INSTANTLY; THE
SOUND REACHES US LATER

This is slow indeed compared to light, which travels at a rate of 186,000 miles per second. Sound travels at different speeds through various materials. Sound travels through rubber only about one fifth as fast as through air, through water about four times as fast, and through iron fifteen times as fast. Sound can travel through some kinds of glass as much as twenty times as fast as it does through air.

21

Sound can travel through an ordinary thread. Get a thread about three feet long. Tie one end around a wooden pencil and loop the other end around a drinking glass. Lift the pencil so that the glass dangles on the thread. As you turn the pencil, the small loop of thread around it will start to turn, then jerk as it slips back again. This jerk will travel along the thread and make the drinking glass ring. Any object has a certain frequency at which it vibrates when

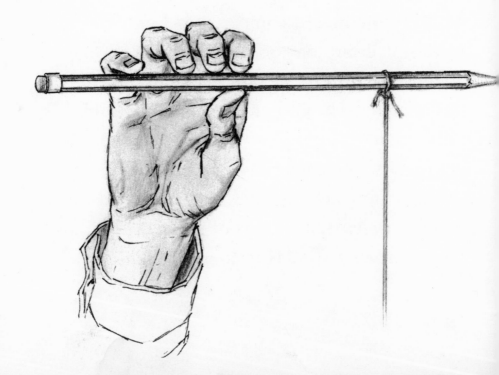

struck, and the glass will ring its note, when it is rubbed, at the same tone, or pitch, as it would have if you had hit it. With practice you can keep the motions of the pencil so small that the ring of the glass will seem very mysterious. You can even make the glass seem to answer questions, using one ring for yes and two rings for no.

THE GLASS WILL SEEM TO RING BY ITSELF!

People have always wanted to send voices over a distance or just from one room to another. At one time a speaking tube was used. If sound is sent into one end of a tube, the sound waves do not have a chance to spread out in all directions, as they ordinarily would. Try speaking into one end of a garden hose while a friend listens at the other end. The sounds can be heard easily, although your friend may be quite far from you. Today doctors still use a stetho-

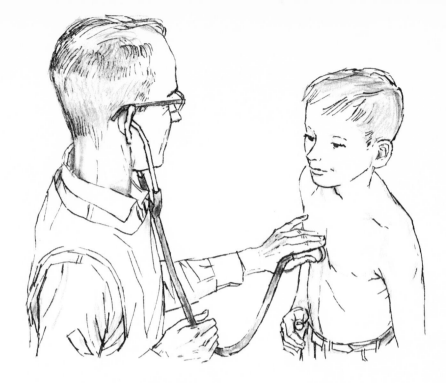

scope, which is simply a tube through which the sounds of a beating heart are sent clearly to the doctor's ears.

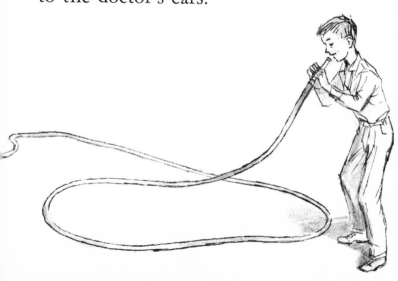

Some people thought that the sounds of speech might be transmitted by an electric current, so that the sound vibrations could be sent long distances over wires. Among these people was Alexander Graham Bell, who came from a family of speech teachers. Bell was very much interested in this idea, for he had seen a device made by a German schoolteacher named Johann Philipp Reis. This gadget was called a

telephone. It sent a vibration over a wire electrically, but the method was imperfect and the resulting vibration at the listening end was more of a noise than a tone. Although this early attempt did not work well, Bell thought that some day an improvement on it might send speech great distances over electric wires.

Even at that time it was known that the vibrations of speech can cause a sheet of paper or other material to vibrate at the same rate as the original sounds. A string telephone, which illustrates this, can be made easily. Run a

thread through a pinhole in the bottom of a paper cup, knotting the thread at one end and fastening it to the bottom of the cup with a piece of tape. Unwind the thread until it is about ten or fifteen feet long and fasten the other end to another cup as you did to the first. When the thread is pulled tight, you can talk

into one cup and be heard by a friend listening at the other one. Even whispers will travel down the thread clearly, if the thread is kept tight, because the bottom of the paper cup acts as a vibrating diaphragm. This diaphragm sends sound vibrations along the thread to the other cup and into the ear of the listener.

Bell also found that a vibrating piece of metal held close to an electromagnet would cause changes in the flow of electricity through the magnet. These changes made the electricity vibrate at the same frequency as the metal, so that the musical tone of the vibrating metal could be sent over the wire. Bell guessed that, if a simple musical tone could be sent this way, a metal diaphragm would transmit all the tones of the human voice. He was right, and after many experiments, his first telephone was shown at the Centennial Exhibition in Philadelphia in 1876. Bell was twenty-nine when the first model of his new invention was demonstrated.

Thomas Edison, a young inventor of exactly the same age, was fascinated by Bell's telephone, and his keen mind saw ways in which it could be improved. Bell's telephone used the same device as both a mouthpiece and an earpiece. Edison developed a separate device for each and used powdered carbon at the diaphragm to change the sound vibrations into electrical impulses. He called it a microphone.

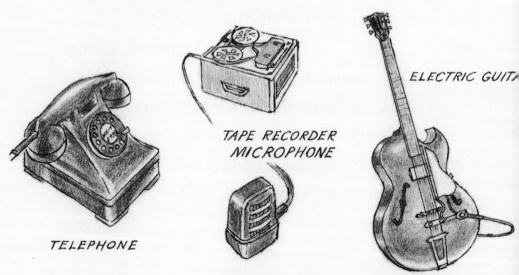

ELECTRIC GUITA

TAPE RECORDER
MICROPHONE

TELEPHONE

USES OF CARBON MICROPHONES

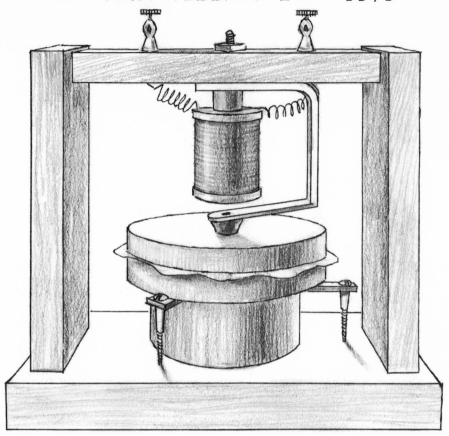

The telegraph had been invented many years earlier, but now Edison invented a way of recording the dot-and-dash signals as dents on a wax roller. His knowledge of the vibrating diaphragm made him think that it must also be

31

possible to record the vibrations produced by voices and music. A needle attached to a diaphragm could make a record of the vibrations when it was pressed against a turning roller of soft material. In 1877, just a year after Bell's invention of the telephone, the first phonograph was built. After wrapping a sheet of tin foil around the roller, Edison spoke into the diaphragm: "Mary had a little lamb, its fleece was white as snow." The needle attached to

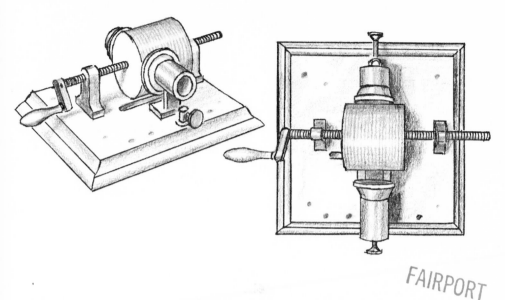

FAIRPORT

the diaphragm transmitted the vibrations onto the tin foil. Edison was as surprised as everyone else when the roller was turned, and the weak but clear sounds of the nursery rhyme were heard again. The mouthpiece of Edison's machine resembled the paper cup used in the string telephone experiment, but the thread attached to the bottom of the cup was replaced by a needle, attached to a diaphragm.

Today, phonographs use electric amplifiers

and loud-speakers to make sounds louder, but Edison's machines used a large funnel-shaped horn, something like a cheerleader's megaphone. To prove how easily the sounds of a record can be magnified, roll a sheet of paper into a cone. Stick a pin through the point of the cone and hold the point of the pin on a

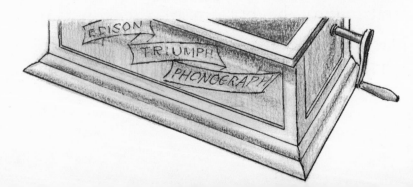

turning record with a little pressure from one finger. Choose an old record (preferably a 78 rpm record, which has the widest grooves), so nothing will be lost if the surface is scratched. The vibrations picked up by the pin will make the paper cone vibrate, and the music of the record will come out of the cone as if by magic. You are producing sounds in the same way that Edison's phonograph did.

Echoes and "Silent" Sounds

Echoes are always fascinating. Have you ever spoken into a deep well or shouted inside a cave? Your voice bounces back once, twice, perhaps many times before the sound is gone.

In a large concert hall there are many echoes.

IRREGULAR CEILING IN BROADCAST THEATER SCATTERS SOUNDS

ACOUSTIVANES OPEN OR CLOSE TO TRAP OR REFLECT SOUND.

Sound is reflected from the walls and the ceiling, so that even a short musical note will seem to ring in the air a long time after the original tone has stopped. Musicians call this type of echo reverberation. Rugs and drapes absorb sounds. Even the seats and people in a concert hall absorb sounds. So an empty theater echoes more than one that is filled with people.

In Salt Lake City, Utah, there is a large tabernacle. It has one of the largest pipe organs in the world and a choir of 378 voices. Because of the gradually curved walls and ceilings, almost all of the sounds are reflected many times, and even the softest sound can be heard anywhere in the building. The choir and organ sound rich and full because of the many reflections of their sounds.

Sometimes echoes behave in very peculiar ways. In the Museum of Science and Industry

in Chicago there is a room called a whispering gallery. This room is part of an ellipsoid, with the ceiling curved like an eggshell. There are two centers called focal points. The walls and ceiling curve in such a way that two people, one standing at each focal point, can whisper softly yet hear each other very well. As one person whispers, all the reflected sound waves,

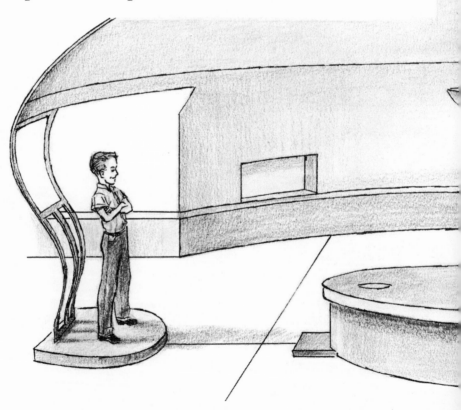

amplified many times louder than seems possible, reach the other person at the same instant.

With a piece of string, a pencil, and two thumbtacks we can easily make a drawing of this type of room. Place a piece of paper on a board and push two thumbtacks into it, leaving a space between them. Tie each end of the

string to one thumbtack so that the string is a little slack. Press the point of the pencil on the paper against the string and stretch it tight. Move the pencil around the thumbtacks, keeping it firmly pressed against the string. You will have to be careful not to catch the string on the thumbtacks.

Your drawing will show the shape of the walls of the whispering gallery, and the thumbtacks indicate the places where the two persons must stand to make their whispers heard. The string, stretched out to any point on the wall, shows the path of a sound wave traveling from

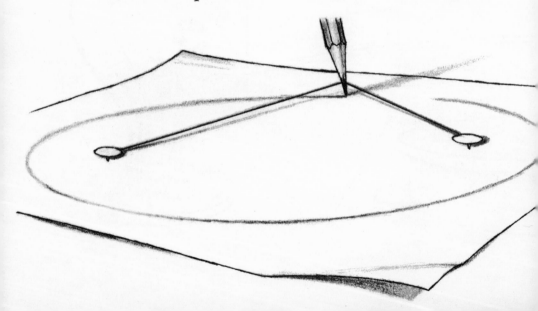

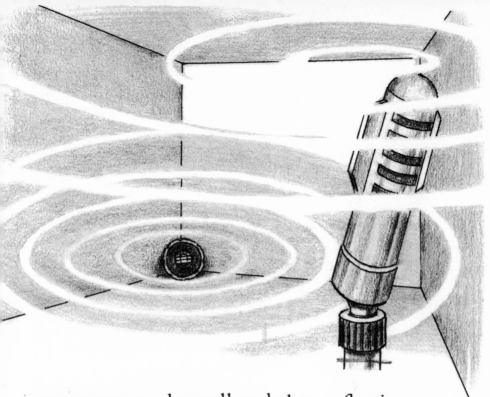

one person to the wall and then reflecting to the other person.

Many broadcasting studios use an empty room, with a loud-speaker at one end and a microphone at the other, to create echoes. Voices or music are piped to the loud-speaker, which in turn sends the sounds into the empty room, where they are reflected many times and then picked up by the microphone. After a

radio announcer's voice goes through this room, it sounds as if he is shouting in a large cave. In the same way, music played by a group of musicians in a small room can have artificial reverberation added, until it seems as if the musicians are performing in a large concert hall.

With a piano, you can make an effect which will seem like an echo, although it works on a different principle. Lift the lid and have someone hold down the loud pedal, so the strings are free to vibrate. Hold your head as close to the strings as possible, and sing or speak into the piano. The strings that match the tones you have made will vibrate, because the sound waves from your voice will strike them. A string's response to another source of vibrations of its own pitch is called resonance. The strings will continue to vibrate after you have stopped speaking or singing and will seem to echo your voice!

All sounds are not as pleasant as voices or music. If a sound does not contain the quality and basic pitch of a musical tone, it is called a noise. Noises can be irritating when they are too loud; even a musical sound can cause a

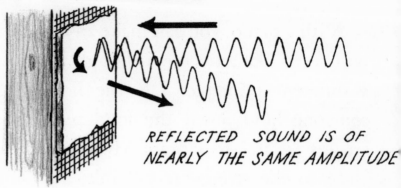

REFLECTED SOUND IS OF
NEARLY THE SAME AMPLITUDE

feeling of pain if it is loud enough. Because of this, people have always tried to find ways to make sounds softer. We have already found that drapes and rugs and clothes can help to destroy sounds. Walls can also be made of special sound-absorbing materials for rooms where echoes are not wanted. Insulated panels, built out from the walls of a room like the dividers of an egg crate, absorb even more sound, because it is trapped in the little boxes formed by the panels. Rooms have now been made that are almost completely soundproof; it is even hard to hear yourself speak in them.

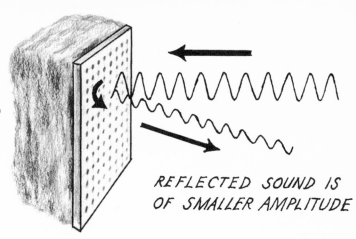

SMALL HOLES IN TRANSITE WALL BOARD ALLOWS SOUND WAVES TO BECOME ABSORBED BY ROCK WOOL BACKING

REFLECTED SOUND IS OF SMALLER AMPLITUDE

An automobile muffler, which helps to eliminate combustion noises inside the motor, uses the same method of deadening sound by trapping it in many compartments.

A surprising group of sounds are those we cannot hear at all. A vibrating object must move back and forth about twenty times per

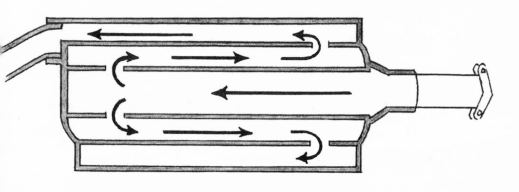

AUTOMOBILE MUFFLER

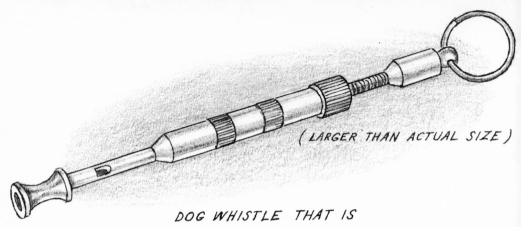

DOG WHISTLE THAT IS
PITCHED TOO HIGH FOR
THE HUMAN EAR TO HEAR

(LARGER THAN ACTUAL SIZE)

second before we can hear a sound. There are also sounds made by very rapid vibrations that we cannot hear. Some people can hear tones as high as 20,000 vibrations per second, but vibrations that create pitches higher than this cannot be detected by the human ear. Dogs can hear higher tones than human beings can; that is why they will respond to a whistle that is pitched so high that we cannot hear it at all. All around us insects make sounds that are too high for us to hear.

Today, scientists are developing ways of using these sounds that we cannot hear. They are called supersonic vibrations and they already have been used to cut diamonds, massage sore muscles, and even drill teeth without pain.

Music and voices are not the only important sounds. Some sounds are able to do useful jobs for us even though we have never heard them.

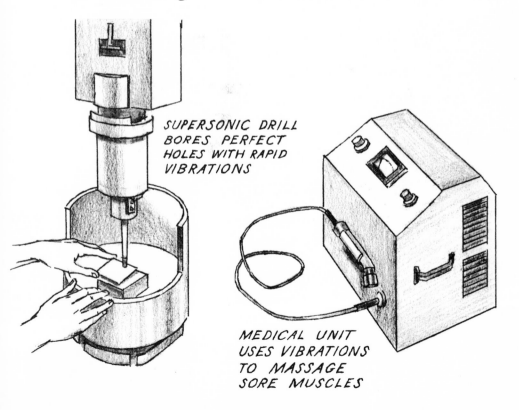

SUPERSONIC DRILL
BORES PERFECT
HOLES WITH RAPID
VIBRATIONS

MEDICAL UNIT
USES VIBRATIONS
TO MASSAGE
SORE MUSCLES

Artificial Sound Effects

Perhaps the most interesting sounds are sound effects. Over the radio we hear the sounds of a gunshot, a forest fire, a thunderstorm, or a freight train. How are these sounds produced? Sometimes the real sound is captured on a record, which is played back on the program later. But many sounds are artificially produced in ways so simple that we can make some of them ourselves.

Several pieces of cellophane crumpled slowly will imitate the sound of an egg frying. A large piece of cellophane crumpled harder can produce the sounds of a forest fire. You will have a great deal of fun if you can use a tape recorder to capture these sounds. Perhaps an interested friend will have one if you do not.

You can make the sound of a steam locomotive with two small sheets of sandpaper glued to two wooden blocks. Slide the sandpaper

sides of the blocks together with a loud, long forward stroke and a soft, short backstroke. This rhythm imitates the accents of the freight engine—*puff* puff *puff* puff. For a passenger train, accent every fourth puff—*puff* puff puff puff *puff* puff puff puff. With just a little practice, you can make the steam locomotive start, stop, climb steep mountains, or fade away into the distance.

On radio broadcasts a gunshot and a whip-crack are often produced in the same way. Two boards about twenty inches long are needed. One board must be sawed into two pieces, five and fifteen inches long. Nail the short piece to one end of the twenty-inch board, and hinge the fifteen-inch piece to it so that it lies on the long board when it is flat. Bring the apparatus down in front of you as if you were cracking a whip. The sharp report will sound very much like a gunshot. Imitating a machine gun is even

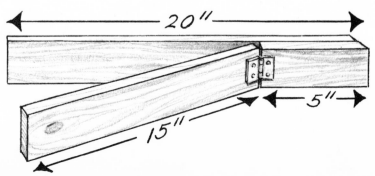

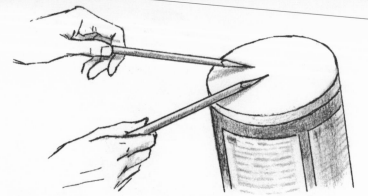

easier. Two wooden pencils tapped rapidly in short bursts on the bottom of an empty oatmeal carton will do nicely.

The National Broadcasting Company in New York has a clever way of producing rain. Inside a glass case a ping-pong ball is suspended in the air. Birdseed falls from a turntable onto the ping-pong ball, strikes a paper cone, and finally lands on a screen. A micro-

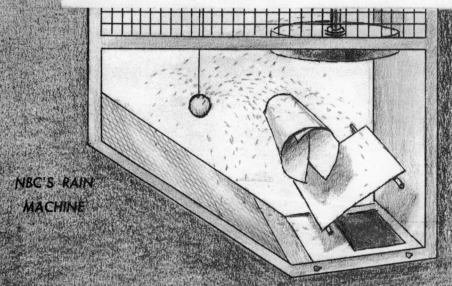

NBC'S RAIN MACHINE

phone near the ping-pong ball picks up and amplifies this perfect imitation of the sound of rain.

You can create the same sound with a box of birdseed, or even a box of rice, and a ping-pong ball. Hold the ball against your ear with one finger and ask someone to hold a handkerchief under it to catch the birdseed. Have the seed poured slowly and steadily against the ping-pong ball. Close your eyes, and it will sound as if you were standing out in an April shower. The handkerchief will catch all the falling birdseed so that there will be no distracting sound when it hits the floor.

You might think that it would be very hard to imitate the sound of marching feet, but a simple device reproduces this sound perfectly. Small blocks of wood about six inches long are hung from a wooden frame about two feet square on strings that cross from one side of the frame to the other. When the frame is raised and lowered, the wooden blocks strike the table like the feet of marching soldiers.

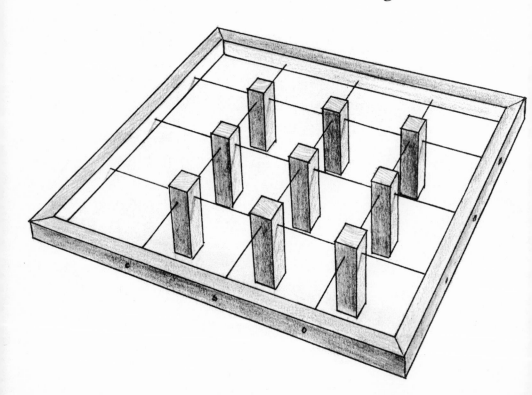

Any sound-effects studio will have a gravel box. It is used to make the sound of a trotting horse. The sound-effects man beats the halves of a coconut shell against the gravel in the rhythm of a trot or a gallop. The sound of a horse trotting on a cobblestone street can be

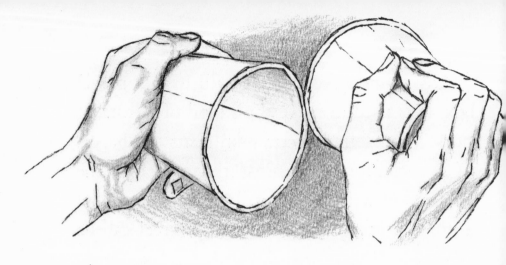

made with two paper cups. Hold one in each hand with the open ends together. Swing your hands up and down, brushing the open ends together, and you will produce a very lifelike sound of horses' hoofs on cobblestones.

You can imitate the sound of thunder with a large sheet of tin. Shake it or strike it with a soft hammer, and the rumbling sound is like the roll of thunder in the distance. Recently a way has been found to create the sound of thunder even more accurately. A screen door, hung inside a large wooden frame, is struck or shaken just like the tin. The sound of the screen is so faint that it is made louder electrically. The next time you walk by a screen door, place your ear close to it and give the screen a tap. The sound will not be strong, but it will be like the thunder of a storm gathering in the distance.

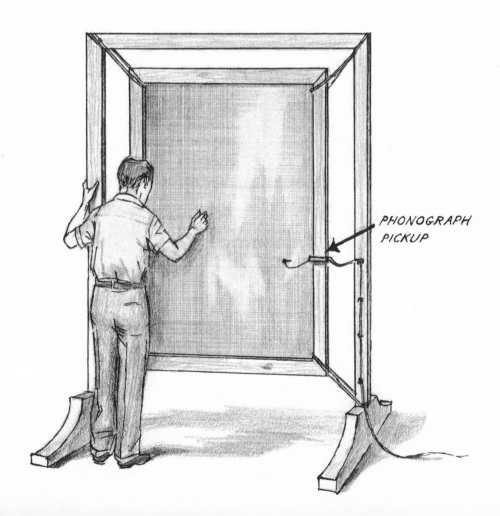

PHONOGRAPH
PICKUP

The strings of a piano can be used to make strange, otherworldly sounds. You will need a feather or a piece of face tissue for the experiment. Lift the lid of the piano and hold down the loud pedal, just as you did to make the piano echo your voice. Rub the tissue or feather back and forth lightly over the strings. The sounds will be spooky and mysterious. If you are using a tape recorder to add some fun to

the experiments, you can record these strange unearthly sounds by holding the microphone close to the piano strings. The sounds are even more surprising when they are played back, because they don't sound like a piano at all.

The noise of a rocking chair or a creaking door can be made with a paper cup. Use a cup that does not have a coating of wax, such as

those used for serving hot coffee. Bend the mouth of the cup flat. Clamp the sides together and slide them back and forth very slowly with your thumb and finger. Hold the cup close to your ear and you will hear a squeaking noise. Keep the squeaks even and they will sound like a rocking chair. One extra-long squeak will imitate a rusty door opening mysteriously.

Fascinating natural sounds are all around us. Some people are able to imitate the sounds of birds or animals. Others, using a microphone and a special sound reflector, have recorded natural sounds on tape. In the musical story, *Peter*

and the Wolf by Prokofiev, the composer has shown how well instruments can reproduce sounds that represent the actions and feelings of his characters. The quack of a duck is imitated by the oboe, the song of a bird by the flute. Every day we hear sounds that remind

us of other sounds. Listen carefully for what is special about each sound, and your imagination will give you ideas for sound effects. Most sounds can be imitated in simple ways, but no sound effect can really replace any of the wonderful sounds of nature.